KT-555-845

Under, over, by the clover

What is a Preposition?

Preposition:
A word that
connects a noun
or pronoun to
other words
in a sentence.

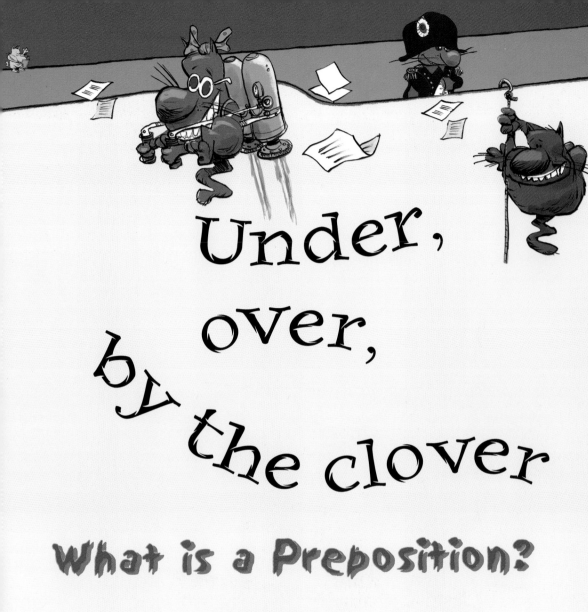

Under, over, by the clover

What is a Preposition?

by Brian P. Cleary
illustrated by Brian Gable

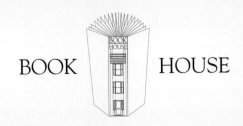

BOOK   HOUSE

Prepositions show us where,

Like in your bed,

beside the chair -

Under,

over,

by the

clover,

About,
above,
or next to
rover.

They tell us time and also place,

During break-time,

after school,

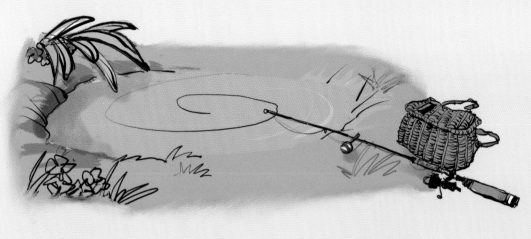

and
between
the pond
and pool.

Ever since the olden days,
there's been a silly myth

That prepositions aren't correct to end a sentence with.

But write your
sentence carefully
and you'll discover that

Ending
with a
preposition

is often where

it's at.

Prepositions
point the
way,

Like, doctors rushed
to where Sue lay.

Or Charlie danced
the Charleston
over on the green,

Down, beyond,
around the
bend,
along the
old ravine.

Across
the
bay

towards
Mississippi,

Through
the yard
of Chris, the hippy.

Relating Nouns
and pronouns

BY

to the other words
and phrases.

Like, Paul's from Pittsburgh,

way up there,

I hid beneath
the old oak chair -

Into, inside, from the zoo,

Home by
way of
Timbuktu.

They tell
the whens,
the wheres,
the hows,

'Cause that's their special mission,

They help to link the other words –

and that's a preposition!

So, what is a preposition?

Do you know?

AUTHOR: BRIAN P. CLEARY is the author of several other books for children, including *To root, to toot, to parachute: What is a Verb?*

ILLUSTRATOR: BRIAN GABLE lives and works in Toronto, Ontario, with his wife Teresa and two children, Kristin and Steven.

Text copyright © 2002 by Brian Cleary
Illustrations copyright © 2002 by Brian Gable
First published in the U.S.A. in 2002 by Carolrhoda Books, Inc.,
a division of Lerner Publishing Group. All rights reserved.

The Salariya Book Company Ltd MMIII
All rights reserved. No part of this book may be reproduced, stored in
a retrieval system or transmitted in any form or by any means, electronic,
mechanical, photocopying, recording or otherwise, without the written
permission of the copyright owner.

Published in Great Britain in 2003 by
Book House, an imprint of
The Salariya Book Company Ltd
25 Marlborough Place, Brighton BN1 1UB

Please visit the Salariya Book Company at:
www.salariya.com
www.book-house.co.uk

ISBN 1 904194 60 5

A catalogue record for this book is available from the British Library.

Printed and bound in USA.